Comptroller of the Currency
Administrator of National Banks

Washington, DC 20219

Futures Commission Merchant Activities

November 1995

Futures Commission Merchant Activities

Table of Contents

Introduction	1
Background	1
Board and Senior Management Oversight	4
Risks Associated with FCMs	9
Examination Objectives	24
Examination Procedures	25
Internal Control Questionnaire	41
Appendix — Sample FCM Request Letter	42

Background

A national bank generally establishes a futures commission merchant (FCM) operating subsidiary for one of two reasons. First, a FCM operating subsidiary provides a bank that engages in futures and options transactions with more direct access to these markets, thereby improving information flow and reducing transaction costs. Second, establishing a FCM operating subsidiary allows a national bank to provide an additional service — that of executing and/or clearing futures and options contracts — to bank customers.

Under 12 USC 24(7) and other statutes, a national bank may establish or acquire and operate an operating subsidiary, including a FCM, to engage in activities that are part of, or incidental to, the business of banking. A FCM operating subsidiary typically solicits or accepts orders to purchase or sell financial or commodity futures contracts and options on these contracts on major exchanges. With respect to national bank operating subsidiaries, "financial futures" include those futures contracts and options on futures contracts relating to assets that a national bank may purchase for its own account; that is, United States securities and United States government agency securities; domestic and Eurodollar money market instruments; bank certificates of deposit, foreign currencies; and gold, silver, platinum and palladium. "Commodity futures" include futures contracts and options on futures contracts for all other financial (equities) and non-financial (agricultural, petroleum, and metals) assets.

A FCM may extend credit or accept money, securities, or property to margin, guarantee, or secure any trades or contracts resulting from its solicitation, acceptance, or execution of orders. A FCM may act as intermediary between a customer and exchange members that actually execute or clear trades. Additionally, a FCM may be a member of an exchange and serve as a clearing member. Operating subsidiaries may offer advisory services, including financial and market analysis, strategy development, research, and discretionary funds management in connection with its FCM activities. The Office of the Comptroller of the Currency (OCC) also permits FCM operating subsidiaries to obtain membership in domestic and foreign futures and options exchanges, clearinghouses, and to register with relevant monetary authorities.

A national bank that intends to establish or acquire a FCM operating subsidiary, or to perform a new activity in an existing FCM subsidiary, generally must submit an application and obtain prior OCC approval under the procedures set forth in 12 CFR Part 5. National bank FCM operating subsidiaries are subject to examination and supervision by the OCC. Unless otherwise provided by statute or regulation, all provisions of federal banking laws and regulations that would apply to the parent national bank shall apply to the operations of the bank's operating subsidiary.

Domestic FCMs are also subject to the Commodity Exchange Act (CEA), as well as rules and regulations issued by the Commodity Futures Trade Commission (CFTC), the National Futures Association (NFA) (a self-regulatory organization), and relevant exchanges. National bank FCM operating subsidiaries that engage in transactions on foreign futures and options exchanges will need to ensure compliance with the laws, rules and regulations of the applicable jurisdiction. (Guidance in this booklet focuses primarily on FCM activities as they relate to domestic exchanges).

Specific OCC conditions that an examiner reviewing a bank's FCM should be aware of include:

- The operating subsidiary shall comply with OCC Banking Circular 277, "Risk Management of Financial Derivatives" (October 27, 1993).

- Loans by the parent to, or any investment of the parent bank in, the operating subsidiary (and its partnership interests) in the aggregate may not exceed the legal lending limit at the time of the loan or investment. The parent bank shall not make investments of equity capital in the operating subsidiary (or its partnership interest) that exceed the lending limit without the OCC's prior written consent. For the purpose of calculating the lending limit in accordance with this investment limitation, the parent bank's investment in the operating subsidiary is deemed unsecured.

- The parent bank may lend the operating subsidiary (or its partnership interest) an additional 10 percent of the parent bank's unimpaired capital and surplus if secured by readily marketable collateral as provided in 12 USC 84.

- The operating subsidiary will not join any exchange or clearing association that requires the parent bank or any other subsidiary of the parent bank to guarantee or otherwise become liable for trades executed and/or cleared by the subsidiary, other than for those trades executed and/or cleared for and on behalf of the bank and any of its affiliates or other operating subsidiaries.

- The operating subsidiary will not become a clearing member of any exchange or clearing association that requires the parent bank to also become a member of that exchange or clearing association unless the parent bank obtains a waiver of the membership requirement.

- The parent bank shall not guarantee or assume responsibility for any liability of its operating subsidiary, other than for those trades executedand/or cleared for and on behalf of the bank and any of its affiliates or other operating subsidiaries.

Futures contracts must be traded on an organized exchange. In the United States, pit trading — or trading that takes place in designated areas or "pits," — is the predominant form, although screen-based trading systems (Globex, Project A, and NYMEX ACCESS) are having some limited success. According to the CEA, which authorizes the CFTC to oversee the futures markets, trading in futures contracts must be "open and competitive." This means that futures contracts are traded by a system of "open outcry"; that is, all orders must be competitively bid and offered (exposed) in the pit (or over the screen-based system).

Consistent with this requirement, under exchange rules, trading may take place only during the official trading hours in pits or over a network using dedicated terminals. Prearranged trades, off-floor negotiation of trades, and crossing of orders held, are examples of noncompetitive trades strictly prohibited under the CEA.

A futures exchange is a voluntary nonprofit organization of its members. Members have a right to trade on the exchange, to have a voice in the exchange's operation, and to sell their memberships. The exchanges are responsible for maintaining records to monitor trading and must be able to construct an audit trail to detect and deter violations of applicable rules and regulations.

The main players in the futures market are: associated persons, introducing brokers, commodity trading advisors (CTAs), floor traders, floor brokers, and customers. With the exception of customers, all of these market participants are required to register with the CFTC (or the NFA, where appropriate), and to comply with certain minimum capital and financial requirements. They also must maintain extensive records as required by the CFTC or the futures exchanges, and they must comply with various reporting requirements.

Associated persons are individuals affiliated with FCMs, introducing brokers, or CTAs who can solicit or accept customers' orders and funds for the purpose of trading. CTAs are in the business of providing advice, either directly or through publications, in writing or through the electronic media, on futures trading or options on futures trading. Floor brokers purchase and sell contracts for their own account and on behalf of customers, while floor traders buy and sell only for their own accounts. Introducing brokers solicit or accept contracts for future delivery, but do not accept money or collateral to margin, guarantee, or secure trades.

Individuals trading in the market fall into two categories: exchange members trading for their own accounts or representatives of trading firms acting as brokers and trading on behalf of customers. Further distinction can be made, based upon the nature of the trading strategy. "Hedgers" are market participants who engage in futures transactions to offset current, or expected, positions in cash markets. "Speculators" are those market participants willing to assume the risk offset by hedgers, with expectations that future price movements will prove profitable. Speculators can further be distinguished by the length of time a position is held: scalpers (seconds or minutes), day traders, and position traders. Scalpers make it easy for brokers to accomplish their trades, because they stand ready to buy from anyone who wants to sell and to sell to anyone who wants to buy. These short-term traders hope to profit from transitory price movements, or from buying at the lower bid and selling at the higher offer, even though spreads in the futures markets are very small (one or two tics). Without the scalpers, the futures markets would be far less liquid and more costly to trade.

Board and Senior Management Oversight

The safe and sound operation of a FCM operating subsidiary is contingent upon effective bank board and senior management oversight. It is incumbent upon the bank's board and senior management to understand the role the FCM plays within the overall business strategies of the bank and the mechanisms used to manage inherent risks.

To fulfill its responsibilities, the bank's board must ensure that appropriate written policies and strong control processes are guiding the actions of the FCM's management. Strong risk management and audit functions are critical to ensuring that actions taken by the FCM's management are consistent with the strategies approved by the bank's board. In addition, effective oversight reduces the likelihood that activities of the FCM may expose the bank to litigation, financial loss, or otherwise damage the bank's reputation.

Policies and Procedures

The bank's board must endorse written corporate policies that provide a framework for the management of risk. As with other complex areas of banking, written policies and procedures are necessary for FCM operating subsidiaries to ensure proper identification, measurement, monitoring, and control of risk exposures.

The board should ensure that the policy framework identifies managerial oversight, assigns clear responsibility, and requires the development and implementation of sufficiently detailed procedures to guide the FCM's daily activities. Policies should detail the type and nature of the activity authorized, articulate the risk tolerance of the bank through comprehensive risk limits, and require regular, independent risk position and performance reporting.

The board should review and endorse significant changes to policies. At least annually, the board, or a committee thereof, also should approve key policy statements, particularly those related to risk tolerance and limits. Meeting minutes should document these actions.

Risk Management

Risk management is the process through which the various risk exposures are identified, measured, monitored, and controlled. The risk management process serves as a communication tool for senior management and the board when evaluating whether management actions are consistent with board strategic objectives. The fundamental elements comprising risk management are: exposure limit systems, risk measurement capabilities, risk monitoring and reporting mechanisms, and segregation of critical operational and control processes. The board and senior management must provide adequate resources (financial, technical expertise, and systems technology) to implement effectively these elements.

Banks establishing a FCM operating subsidiary must possess risk control functions commensurate with the extent and complexity of the FCM's activities. The underlying risks associated with FCM activities are not new to banking, although their measurement and control can be more complex than for other traditional products or activities. For example, measuring credit risk in futures transactions involves consideration of margin determination and collection, issues not common to direct lending or over-the-counter (OTC) derivatives transactions. Therefore, the OCC considers a strong risk control function to be critical. The OCC considers the lack of an adequate risk control function, relative to the level of bank FCM operating subsidiary activity, to be an unsafe and unsound banking practice.

The OCC expects banks with a FCM operating subsidiary to ensure the effective operation of an independent risk control function. This function should be a separate unit — it need not be standalone for the FCM and may perform risk control activities for other areas of the bank — reporting directly to executive management, the board, or a designated committee thereof. The risk control function should perform independent evaluations of risk-taking activities on an ongoing basis. These evaluations would include assessing the propriety of risk levels and the adequacy of the risk management processes. The risk control function should monitor the development and implementation of applicable control policies and risk measurement systems. Observations should be periodically communicated to senior management and the board.

Risk Measurement

Accurate measurement of FCM-related risks is necessary for proper management and control. Risk measurement at the board and senior management levels is generally accomplished on a portfolio basis and aggregated according to type of risk. At a line management level, risk may be more appropriately measured by product, market factor, or other characteristics. All significant risks should be measured and considered in the assessment of risk on a bankwide basis. For example, measuring credit risk at the bank level should also take into consideration exposures arising from activities of the FCM operating subsidiary.

Management should recognize that measurement of some types of risk is an approximation. Certain risks, such as liquidity risk, can be difficult to quantify and can vary with economic and market conditions. At a minimum, the board and management should assess the FCM's vulnerability to each risk associated with futures and options activities, on an ongoing basis, in response to changing circumstances. The sophistication and precision of risk measurement methods will necessarily vary by the types and volumes, as well as the riskiness, of activities undertaken.

Risk Limits

The board of directors should approve aggregate risk-taking limits at least once a year. Limits should be directly related to the nature of the bank's strategies, historical performance, and the overall level of earnings or capital that the board is willing to place at risk. An effective risk management process will also ensure that the board reassesses limits when necessary, with appropriate revisions made to reflect changes in resources or market conditions. For example, in periods of abnormal market volatility, the board may request FCM management to lower open interest limits, so as to reduce liquidity risk exposure to the FCM.

In addition to providing a means of control over aggregate exposure, the board and senior management should use limits and exposure measurement systems to foster communication of changes in the FCM's overall risk profile. Bank senior management should require FCM managers to be accountable for adhering to limits. FCM management should also promptly report unanticipated changes and progressively deteriorating positions, as well as other significant issues arising in their positions, to the risk control function and responsible management. Reports from risk control units to senior management or the board should never disclose a breach of limits that business managers have not previously reported.

When establishing the FCM operating subsidiary's overall limit structure, bank senior management and the board should consider the interrelationship between risk assumed by the FCM and risk assumed by other affiliates (including the bank). The nature of bank operating subsidiary FCMs is such that the primary risk exposures at the FCM will be related to credit and operational issues. Because credit and operational risk are affected by changes in price risk and liquidity, senior management and the board should evaluate the probability and impact of market events, counterparty defaults, or other financial scenarios which might impact the business of the FCM, directly or indirectly, through a contagion effect.

Evaluation of Risk Versus Return

Fundamental to an analysis of risk-taking is an assessment of return. This risk/return analysis should reflect the purpose or intent of management when establishing a FCM operating subsidiary. For each capacity in which a FCM might function (nonmember, executing member, or clearing member), the risks are slightly different and the return should be analyzed accordingly.

The return on capital invested in a FCM operating subsidiary is typically derived from three sources: commissions from trades, commissions from clearing services (as applicable), and savings realized from executing and clearing trades for the parent bank and affiliates (as applicable). The proportion each of these sources contributes to the overall return on bank-invested capital will depend on the strategic and business objectives of the FCM and the parent bank.

When orders are accepted, the customer is charged a fee. The fee includes a transaction processing fee, an exchange fee, the clearinghouse fee, and some additional increment to compensate the FCM for market access services. A nonmember FCM passes along the exchange, clearinghouse, and floor broker fees via payments made to the member FCM used to execute and/or clear the customer's requested trade, as appropriate. Alternatively, a FCM which is an exchange member itself will incur all the risks and associated costs derived from serving in a trade execution and clearing capacity; in return, it will earn the full amount of the fee charged to the customer. A FCM that executes and/or clears trades for the parent bank or affiliate provides a return to capital by eliminating the fees paid to another FCM for executing and clearing futures and options on futures transactions.

Regardless of the revenue-generating strategy, the risk/return analysis should provide the board and senior management with meaningful information about levels of risk and adequacy of return. The volume of FCM activities and dedication of resources to these activities should determine the level of sophistication needed for the risk/return analyses.

Ideally, management should measure performance against capital, adjusted for strategic, credit, liquidity, transaction, compliance, and reputation risks confronting the business. All banks with FCM operating subsidiaries should have a method for ensuring that adequate capital is in place to support potential exposures. The evaluation of capital adequacy should extend beyond the determination of compliance with regulatory minimum capital requirements and should consider the amount of capital needed to support the level and complexity of the FCM's risk-taking activities. Such evaluations are useful in assessing performance and ensuring that capital is allocated efficiently.

Audit Coverage

Audit coverage of FCM activities should focus on internal controls and systems reliability. Audit coverage should be provided by professionals such as internal auditors, external auditors, or some combination thereof who have sufficient independence and expertise. Auditors should be knowledgeable of the risks inherent in futures and options on futures trading, executing, and clearing, and the risk management methodologies needed to control these activities. Audit reports should promptly identify and disclose internal control weaknesses and systems deficiencies to FCM management and to bank senior management and the board.

Audit coverage should assess the internal organization of the FCM and identify any organizational weaknesses. The individuals and units performing risk control functions should be independent from the units engaged in the business and trading functions. This separation helps mitigate the risk that arises when the self-interest of an individual employee conflicts with the goals of the FCM or of the parent bank.

Auditors also should conduct compliance testing of FCM activities. (This testing may be performed by the audit team or by the FCM compliance staff). The testing process should evaluate the FCM's compliance with the rules and regulations governing futures activities, in addition to compliance with bank-approved policies and procedures. Bank management should ensure that the audit team selected to review the FCM have the appropriate technical background and expertise to test for compliance with regulatory requirements, which may vary depending on the nature of the FCM's business.

Information Systems

The board should receive information periodically that illustrates exposure trends, the adequacy of, and compliance with, policies, risk limits, and risk/return performance. The frequency and composition of this information should depend upon the nature and significance of the FCM's activities. For example, a FCM engaging solely in futures transactions for risk management purposes by the parent bank or affiliates should focus board reports on clearinghouse risks and risk management effectiveness. On the other hand, a FCM with aggressive customer solicitation practices should ensure the board is kept informed of changes in credit administration practices, margin controls, and compliance procedures used to reduce the likelihood of customer litigation.

Effective management information systems tailor the level of detail to the intended audience, providing greater detail in reports prepared for line management than for senior management or the board. Management directly responsible for risk-taking activities should have reports that provide information in sufficient detail to assess risk, return, and the ability to meet stated objectives.

Affiliates

If a bank establishes a FCM operating subsidiary to broker trades for the bank and other related entities, it is incumbent upon bank senior management and the board to establish a control framework to ensure accurate monitoring of transactions between affiliates and the FCM. The board and senior management should establish policies and procedures that address FCM transactions for affiliates. At a minimum, the policy should describe the nature of acceptable affiliate transactions and require that transactions for customers take priority over the interests of the FCM and its affiliates. Senior management should ensure that affiliate transactions comply with such policy.

Risks Associated with FCMs

For purposes of the OCC's discussion of risk, examiners assess banking risk relative to its impact on capital and earnings. From a supervisory perspective, risk is the potential that events, expected or unanticipated, may have an adverse impact on the bank's capital or earnings. The OCC has defined nine categories of risk for bank supervision purposes. These risks are: Credit, Interest Rate, Liquidity, Price, Foreign Exchange, Transaction, Compliance, Strategic, and Reputation. These categories are not mutually exclusive, any product or service may expose the bank to multiple risks. For analysis and discussion purposes, however, the OCC identifies and assesses the risks separately.

The applicable risks associated with domestic FCM activities are: strategic, reputation, credit, liquidity, transaction and compliance. Generally, bank operating subsidiary FCMs do not assume price risk because they do not trade for their own account. Price risk indirectly impacts a FCM's credit risk however, and this interconnection is discussed further in the credit risk section of this introduction under the discussion of "margin." (If the FCM engages in proprietary trading, the examiner should refer to the price risk management guidance contained in the "Risk Management of Financial Derivatives" booklet of the Comptroller's Handbook.)

Strategic Risk

Strategic risk is the risk to earnings or capital arising from adverse business decisions or improper implementation of those decisions. This risk is a function of the compatibility of an organization's strategic goals, the business strategies developed to achieve those goals, the resources deployed against these goals, and the quality of implementation. The resources needed to carry out business strategies are both tangible and intangible. They include communication channels, operating systems, delivery networks, and managerial capacities and capabilities.

Strategic Risk Management Practices

Strategic risk associated with FCM activities can be controlled if the bank board carefully analyzes what it hopes to achieve by establishing a FCM subsidiary and by requiring ongoing communication between FCM management and senior management and the board of the parent bank. Before establishing a FCM subsidiary, senior management of the parent bank should conduct a cost/benefit analysis to determine how the FCM business will mesh with the corporate strategies of the parent bank. The board and senior management should ensure that adequate resources are dedicated to the FCM for staffing, technical, and operational needs. Once established, the parent bank should establish an oversight framework, similar to that discussed above, that allows the bank to maintain ongoing, independent evaluation of the risks associated with the FCM business.

Reputation Risk

Reputation risk is the risk to earnings or capital arising from negative public opinion. This affects the institution's ability to establish new relationships or services or continue servicing existing relationships. This risk can expose the institution to litigation, financial loss, or damage to its reputation. Reputation risk exposure is present throughout the organization and is why banks have the responsibility to exercise an abundance of caution in dealing with its customers and community. This risk is present in activities such as asset management and agency transactions.

A bank with a FCM operating subsidiary should recognize that the culture fostered by senior management of the FCM will directly impact the amount of reputation exposure faced by the bank. The bank's board should ensure that the management of the FCM possesses the necessary experience in futures trading, brokerage, and operations activities. FCM activities are unlike most other areas of banking. FCM management requires specialized skills and familiarity with the futures industry and with exchanges. Integrating the management styles and philosophies of the futures industry into the banking industry can be difficult. Bank management should ensure that policies and procedures guiding the activities of FCM management direct and reinforce actions which are consistent with the risk profile approved by the board.

While experienced in the technical aspects of the industry, futures industry management may not be familiar with the risk management philosophies common to a typical commercial bank. For example, the transaction-oriented nature of FCM business generally is different from the relationship-oriented nature of commercial banking. When a commercial bank approves a customer transaction for a loan or other extension of credit (for example, an OTC derivative or a letter of credit), the bank considers whether the proposed transaction can meet the financial needs of the customer, whether the customer has the financial wherewithal to engage in the transaction, and whether the customer appears to understand the risks applicable to the proposed transaction. Because commercial banks devote significant resources to building banking relationships with customers which extend far beyond individual transactions, the development and maintenance of customer relationships may have a different priority for the bank than would be typical for a FCM.

The regulated nature of the futures markets makes it likely that FCM management is experienced in issues of sound trade practices. For example, the rules of the CEA and CFTC require a FCM employee to receive ethics training that stresses honest and fair dealing practices which are in the best interest of the customer.

Reputation Risk Management Practices

In some areas, a clear separation of the functions between a bank and its FCM subsidiary is needed to reduce the bank's exposure to losses stemming from potential customer complaints involving the FCM. This separation is designed to offset, as much as possible, damage to the bank's reputation. While a bank and its FCM have a distinct legal status (by separate incorporation), the FCM could wrongly be considered part of the bank by the business community. As a result, it is critical that the FCM employ competent and appropriately trained personnel and that it complies with applicable laws, rules, regulations, guidelines, conditions, policies, and procedures. To protect the bank's reputation, the FCM should implement policies and procedures that address the issues of soliciting new customers, analyzing customer creditworthiness, performing ongoing monitoring of customer accounts, and handling customer complaints.

A FCM should also institute procedures to ensure that customer transactions are authorized and executed in accordance with applicable customer specifications. For example, when a customer of the FCM places a "limit order," the FCM makes a best-effort commitment to bid or offer the customer's order at the specified market price or better. The FCM does not have an obligation to fill the customer order in the case of limit orders. When a FCM customer places a "stop order," however, the FCM has an obligation to execute this order if market prices reach the pre-specified threshold. In either case, the FCM should have procedures that describe mechanisms to track orders according to specific limits or restrictions. Failure to handle orders in a manner consistent with customer specifications may result in the FCM expending capital to cover customer opportunity costs.

Credit Risk

Credit risk is the risk to earnings or capital arising from an obligor's failure to meet the terms of any contract with the bank or otherwise fail to perform as agreed. Credit risk is found in all activities where success depends on counterparty, issuer, or borrower performance. It arises any time bank funds are extended, committed, invested, or otherwise exposed through actual or implied contractual agreements, whether reflected on or off the balance sheet.

The credit risk associated with futures and options on futures differs from that associated with OTC derivatives because of the different institutional environments in which the instruments are traded. While OTC instruments are customized bilateral agreements, futures are standardized, fungible contracts traded on organized exchanges. In order to trade futures, customers must trade through intermediaries.

As noted above, a FCM is an entity that is authorized to receive customers' orders, take margin, and, if it is a member of an exchange, execute orders on the floor of the exchange. If it is a clearing member, it may clear the trade as well. Acting as financial intermediaries, FCMs are exposed to credit risk when they perform these services. The exchanges have implemented certain institutional arrangements which reduce counterparty risk through controls designed to limit the effect of counterparty default. These arrangements include margin requirements, daily marking-to-market of open positions, daily price limits, and an organized clearinghouse.

Margin Requirements

When a futures contract is bought or sold, the position has no value. Subsequent price changes affect the value of the position. Increases in value are profitable for the longs (purchaser of a contract), and unprofitable for the shorts (seller of a contract). With few exceptions, initial margin is required at the initiation of a position. Initial margin serves as a good faith deposit to offset any losses to the intermediary (or the clearinghouse) should the customer default on the trade. To clarify the concept and role of initial margin, it is useful to note that this "performance bond" does not involve any extension of credit, but rather acts as collateral for adverse market movements and subsequent defaults and losses.

Domestically, initial margins are established in relation to historical price volatility, expected market volatility, and whether the transaction involves speculative, hedging or spreading (the simultaneous purchase or sale of one futures contract against the sale or purchase of another futures contract) activities. For example, some domestic exchanges use the implied volatility in the futures contract over the previous one, three, and six months, and absolute dollar price changes, to establish a level of margin that covers approximately the 95th percentile of absolute daily price changes.

Different intermediaries set their margin requirements depending on the function they perform in the marketplace. The futures clearinghouses set levels of margin which their members are required to maintain for any open positions. The exchanges set minimum levels of margin which a member FCM must maintain for positions it carries for itself or for its customers. The FCMs set levels of margin which they require of their customers. Since the levels set by any individual FCM must be at least as large as those required by exchange and/or clearinghouse rules, the ability and willingness to establish higher margin requirements for customers are one way a FCM can control credit exposures.

Daily Marking-to-Market

After the posting of initial margin, price movements may cause an open future or options position to suffer a loss. A decline in the value of a contract will result in the FCM issuing a margin call to the customer. If the initial margin falls below the maintenance margin level, the customer will be required to bring the margin back up to the initial margin level. Should the customer default on the margin call, the FCM has the remaining margin to cover the difference between the price at which the contract is currently trading and its value at the close of the previous day. Because futures contracts are marked-to-market daily, the margin serves to reduce the risk of default from any price change.

Daily Price Limits

Daily price limits are frequently used in domestic nonfinancial futures and options markets to further reduce the risk of large losses. Price limits control credit risk because they constrain the amount of price change in certain contracts on any given day. For example, in crude oil futures trading, daily price changes are limited to $1.50 per barrel. If the price of crude oil contracts fell $1.50, the maximum daily loss for one contract (1,000 barrels) would be $1,500. Similarly, if the price of crude oil contracts increased $1.50, the maximum daily loss for a trader who was short one contract would be $1,500.

The Clearinghouse

One advantage of exchange-traded instruments over customized OTC instruments is that the clearinghouse is interposed as the counterparty to all transactions. When a FCM sends a customer's order to the exchange floor and that order is executed against the order of another FCM, the clearinghouse stands between the two FCMs to guarantee the trade. Thus, the buyer buys from the clearinghouse, and the seller sells to the clearinghouse. The clearing member substitutes its credit for that of its customers and, thereby, assumes the full risk of its customers' defaults up until the time of delivery on a matured contract. Clearing members make margin deposits to the clearinghouse and assume full financial and performance responsibility for every trade presented to the clearinghouse — regardless of whether the position is carried for a customer's account, the account of another exchange member, or for the clearing member's proprietary account.

Clearinghouses mitigate the risk of default through self-insurance programs designed to cover losses should one or more of their members become insolvent. Depending on the structure of the clearinghouse, members are required either to contribute to a guarantee fund, or to purchase stock in a clearing corporation. In the event of default of one of its members, the clearinghouse would look first to the margins and other assets of the defaulting member to satisfy net margin payable to other clearing members. If this is insufficient, the clearinghouse would draw on the guarantee fund or on the capital of the clearing corporation. It is in this sense that the risk is shared or spread among the clearing members.

Some clearinghouses use a net margin system in which the clearing FCM's margin obligation is determined by the net of its long and short positions. Other clearing associations use a gross margin system which requires clearing members to post full margin for each long and each short position. Gross margin systems provide greater stability to the clearinghouse since the required margin level is higher than under a net margin system. Net margining reduces the aggregate margin balance held at the clearinghouse and may place greater reliance on the guarantee fund.

Credit Risk Management Practices

Clearinghouses manage credit risk by:

•   Establishing minimum capital requirements for the clearing members.

•   Assuring that clearing members' post initial and variation margin promptly.

- Monitoring the financial condition of its members.

- Overseeing members' positions on a daily basis.

Clearinghouses also manage their exposure by monitoring members' accounts on a daily basis, by conducting exchange audits, and by performing other compliance functions.

FCMs rely on margin requirements and credit administration practices to protect themselves from credit losses. With respect to margin, a FCM should have policies that direct the timely liquidation or close out of under-margined positions. Credit administration practices should be guided by policies that address customer selection, account documentation, and the determination of creditworthiness. FCMs can use the customer selection process to reduce the likelihood of loss from customer default. For example, they may agree to deal only with those bank customers assigned the highest internal credit ratings.

Proper documentation of customer authority is also critical for controlling credit risk exposures. The FCM should ensure that sufficient authorization has been obtained from the customer prior to execution of futures or options transactions and that transactions are consistent with any restrictions or limitations included in such authorization.

Initial determination of creditworthiness and ongoing credit evaluations are also tools available to the FCM to control credit risk exposures. Credit limits should take into consideration other exposures arising at the parent bank or affiliates and any correlation risks which might arise if the customer transacts futures and options on multiple exchanges. The FCM may rely on the bank's ongoing credit evaluation process to ensure that customers have the financial capacity and liquidity to meet margin requirements both in normal market conditions and during periods of unusual or stressed market conditions. Although the FCM does not need to duplicate bank credit files, it should retain sufficient information to support the determination of creditworthiness.

If the FCM is a clearing member, it may elect to provide clearing services to other FCMs. The account of the non-clearing FCM can either be fully disclosed (in which case the clearing FCM knows the actual customer's identity, position, and margin status) or omnibus (in which case such customer information is not disclosed to the clearing FCM). If a FCM elects to accept omnibus accounts, it should have appropriate procedures in place to ensure that the originating FCM selects creditworthy customers and collects margin according to exchange rules.

Some customers may need or wish to execute through other brokers, known as "give-up brokers." Common reasons for executing through several brokers are to disguise the size of a position or hide the identity of the principal to the transaction. This practice, however, may expose a clearing FCM to risks that are difficult to control. For example, if the customer chooses to execute through other brokers, the clearing FCM may not have the opportunity to reject trades prior to presentation for clearing. If the FCM both executes and clears transactions, however, it would be in a position to evaluate transactions relative to customer account limits. For example, if the customer placed unusual orders or if a series of transactions appeared to pose undue risk, the FCM could question the purpose of such transactions. If necessary, the FCM could refuse to accept the customer's order. For these reasons, some FCMs may prohibit "clearing only" accounts. If the FCM chooses to clear trades executed by others, it may wish to place higher credit qualifications on the customer. Restricting the volume and type of "clearing only" trades, requesting prior notice of "clearing only" trades, or otherwise reducing the exposure to trades that the FCM is unaware of prior to presentation for clearing are other ways in which a FCM can control credit risk.

When considering whether or not to apply for clearing membership, a FCM must assess an exchange and its clearinghouse. Among the factors the FCM should consider are the number, and financial strength, of the clearing members, the type of guarantee provided to clearing members, the degree of protection afforded by margins (gross versus net), the frequency and cause of member defaults in the past, the quality of supervision over executing and clearing members, and the reliability of accounting statements for the clearinghouse and its members.

Examiners need to recognize that the guarantees between the clearinghouse and its members do not extend to customers. To protect customers from the risk of loss resulting from the failure or default of a FCM, exchanges have adopted customer protection rules. Exchanges require strict segregation of customer funds from FCM funds. This rule will not help customers if their margin must be used to cover the default of another customer of the same FCM, however. For example, in 1985, Volume Investors (a FCM and clearing member of the Commodity Exchange, Inc.) defaulted because of the failure of a large customer (the customer could not meet a margin call after a significant change in the price of gold futures). The clearinghouse only guaranteed the trades between Volume and other clearing members. The margin of some non-defaulting Volume customers was used by the clearinghouse to meet the financial requirements of this guarantee.

A FCM is exposed to this risk if it elects not to be a clearing member of an exchange, but instead decides to utilize the services of a clearing member. The FCM is then "just another customer," with its margin at the clearing FCM subject to possible use for covering losses resulting from the default of another customer of the clearing FCM.

Furthermore, examiners should understand that exchange minimum margins and daily price limits do not eliminate credit risk. Intra-day price movements may occur so rapidly that the FCM cannot call and receive sufficient variation margin. Additionally, successive daily price moves may eventually cause losses so extensive that a customer is unable to meet obligations and, consequently, defaults. FCMs must take additional controls to reduce these risks. A first step is the careful selection of customers who understand the risks of futures and options on futures trading and have the financial strength to fulfill their contracts. Secondly, FCMs should establish customer credit limits that are appropriate for the account. Bank subsidiary FCMs commonly restrict their customer base to large corporations, other financial institutions, and fund managers. If the FCM accepts customer accounts from entities that are not existing bank customers, the FCM and/or its parent bank should develop well-defined credit standards. The customer selection criteria should specify whether the FCM would accept accounts from corporate clients, hedge funds, trusts, or individuals.

Liquidity Risk

Liquidity risk is the risk to earnings or capital arising from a bank's inability to meet its obligations when they come due without incurring unacceptable losses. Liquidity risk includes the inability to manage unplanned decreases or changes in funding sources. Liquidity risk also arises from the bank's failure to recognize or address changes in market conditions that affect the ability to liquidate assets quickly and with minimal loss in value.

Cash Flow Liquidity

Cash flow liquidity involves the ability to fund the operating needs of the FCM at a reasonable cost. As noted previously, a primary source and use of funds for a FCM is the receipt and payment of margin. As FCM customers place futures orders, they are required to provide a margin to the FCM which becomes a source of cash flow. As the FCM places the order at the exchange, however, the clearinghouse will require margin of the FCM, which then becomes a use of cash flow for the FCM.

The timing of clearinghouse cash flow requirements is not under the control of the FCM because exchanges mark-to-market daily and require that margins be maintained on a daily basis. Since FCMs have a clear obligation to collect margin from their customers, however, the FCM has some flexibility with respect to the timing of such cash flows. Subject to CFTC and exchange grace period restrictions and capital requirements, a FCM may deviate from the practice of domestic exchanges that require daily mark-to-market and margin calls. Cash flow may become a liquidity issue, however, if a FCM customer fails to meet a margin call, requiring the FCM to fund the customer's position until margin can be made or the position closed out.

Product Liquidity

Product liquidity involves the ability to trade an asset quickly at a price that is fair and reasonable in light of underlying demand and supply conditions. In other words, trading at fair prices.

When an exchange proposes to trade a futures contract, it must first submit it to the CFTC for review. One important criterion that enters into the review is the potential demand for the product. The concern is that if the demand is not sufficient, the market will not be liquid. When a contract fails to attract sufficient trading interest, it is said to "fail." Liquidity requires a significant number of market participants who see economic use in the contract. In an illiquid market, it may take time to unwind a position, or the trader may only be able to do so at a high cost. Additionally, in an illiquid market, the market price may be hard to determine.

Liquidity risk is generally lower in the futures markets than it is in the OTC derivatives market where a market and a market price for an exotic instrument may not exist. In periods of market stress, however, all markets may be illiquid. On October 19, 1987, for example, enormous sell pressure in the futures, cash, and securities markets took place. One of the reasons for the steep market drop was that there were no buyers. If one side of the market is absent, no market exists — or it is essentially illiquid.

Liquidity Risk Management

Cash flow liquidity is a primary risk to FCM operations and can best be managed through the implementation of procedures that are designed to minimize unexpected mismatched payments and settlements. Additionally, concentration limits that reduce the reliance on any individual or related entities also serves to control the FCM's exposure to liquidity risk.

One way to limit liquidity risk is through a customer margin collection practice which parallels the daily mark-to-market practice of the clearinghouse. If customer margins are collected on a daily basis, it is unlikely that the FCM will find itself in a position where it has advanced margin to the clearinghouse before collecting margin from a customer. A FCM that does not adopt margin collection practices which parallel those of the exchange should be prepared to demonstrate, to examiners, controls addressing this potential cash flow liquidity exposure.

Concentration limits may also be used to control the vulnerability of FCMs to cash flow imbalances. If the composition of the FCM customer base is such that an interruption in the cash flow of any individual customer is insignificant relative to the total cash flows of the FCM, liquidity risk should be reduced. Furthermore, if the futures contracts acquired for FCM customers are well diversified, it is less likely that a market event will affect the cash flow abilities of each of the customers in the same manner.

Finally, product liquidity can be controlled with policies and procedures that specify approved contract types and tenors. Such policies should consider factors such as contract "open interest" (the total number of futures contracts that have not been eliminated by either an offsetting trade or by delivery) and the market "depth" (the number of market participants buying and selling contracts).

Transaction Risk

Transaction risk is the risk to earnings or capital arising from problems with service or product delivery. This risk is a function of internal controls, information systems, employee integrity, and operating processes. Transaction risk exists in all products and services.

An important aspect of FCM activities involves the executing and clearing of trades. Whether the FCM performs these functions for its own account, the account of affiliates, or for customers, the FCM must process transactions accurately and quickly, at a reasonable cost.

Transaction Flow

When a customer decides to enter an order, the customer calls either a FCM or an introducing broker to take the order. Since an introducing broker will merely transmit the order to a FCM for handling, this discussion will focus on the activity of FCMs. The person who takes the order generally will be an associated person or merely an order entry clerk. (In certain cases, the FCM may allow the customer to call directly to the floor trader.) The order will be time-stamped and have the customer's name and account number attached. Unless called to the floor trader directly, the order will then be phoned or otherwise transmitted to the FCM's office on the trading floor. Runners then communicate the order to a floor broker in the pit who is employed by the FCM. Often this "communication" of the order takes place by hand signals. The broker will loudly bid or offer the order to the pit (or accept the bid or offer of another trader).

Once the order is filled, the broker records the price, number of contracts, time bracket (the trading day is divided into half-hour time brackets), and opposite broker on a trading card. The broker subsequently signals to the runner that the order is filled, and the runner goes back to the FCM's booth, where confirmation is sent to the customer. The whole process may take less than one minute as the pits are active, especially in the near contract month. (The exchange has separately made a record of the price and time of trade as recorded by the price reporter stationed on the trading floor.) Finally, the

FCM and clearinghouse use the trade cards to reconcile trades and retain an audit trail of transactions.

Transaction Risk Management Practices

A bank FCM should have comprehensive written policies, procedures, and systems covering transaction risk. Policies and procedures should cover the receipt of orders, the execution of orders, trade capture, pay/receive, safekeeping of cash and margin collateral, accounting practices, and the reconcilement process.

Since the quality of operational support depends on the quality of staff, the FCM should address the need to attract and develop capable employees. Compensation plans should be designed to retain experienced, competent operations staff.

CFTC and exchange regulations are designed to promote sound operational practices. For example, CFTC regulations require FCMs to execute trades for customers in a fair and equitable manner. Procedures should ensure that customer order transactions are transmitted and executed fairly, generally in the order received. When executing orders for the FCM's own account or for the account of affiliated entities, procedures should ensure that customer orders for the same contract, executable at or near market prices, are given priority. As such, prompt trade order entry, recording, and tracking are necessary to ensure customer orders executable at or near market prices are transmitted and executed prior to orders for the same contract for the FCM's own account or the account of affiliated entities. For example, regulations require that orders must be time-stamped when received, when transmitted for execution, and when reported out as executed. Controls such as prenumbered tickets or automated tracking systems help to ensure that incoming trade orders are recorded and tracked.

Accounting controls, required by the CFTC and exchange regulations, help to ensure that the FCM keeps current ledgers or accounts showing each transaction affecting assets, liabilities, income, expense, and capital of the firm. For example, where accounts or balances are due to or from other entities (safekeeping agents, payment agents, clearinghouse balances, etc.), the FCM should have accounting procedures that require prompt reconcilements and reports to management of any exceptions. If the FCM executes orders for customers, accounting controls must require prompt recording of orders in customer ledgers and transaction journals and recording of all customer funds or property received from customers. Controls over customer property must ensure proper segregation, identify the location of assets, revalue assets at fair market value, and provide for reconcilements. If the FCM invests customer funds, accounting records must show the amount, type, date of receipt, and earnings on such funds, and such investments must be limited to the types of investments permitted under the CEA and CFTC rules.

Operational controls also should ensure that each transaction is promptly confirmed with the floor broker or trader on the other side of the transaction. Records should include a log of orders received, filled, unfilled, or canceled. Unmatched trades should be promptly investigated. Transactions for customers, including orders for affiliates or associated persons, should be promptly confirmed in writing. Control systems require separation of the following duties: account acceptance, order receipt, execution, confirmation preparation and comparison, margin receipt/delivery, and accounting entries.

Additionally, the FCM should have operational procedures to ensure that trades are fairly allocated when orders are bundled. Under CFTC rules, each order sent to the exchange for execution is required to be linked to a particular account. To accommodate FCMs and CTAs who manage multiple accounts with similar investment goals, an exception to the rule was given for managed accounts. Orders can be "bundled" or grouped together. Once the total bundle is filled in a sequence of transactions, the fills are allocated to individual accounts. The assignment uses one of two methods: a predetermined allocation scheme, or the determination of a volume-weighted average price. The accounts in the bundle have to be specified before the orders are sent to the exchange, and the allocation scheme must remain on file with the member FCM.

Sound controls also include systems to track errors and discrepancies. Customer complaints should be thoroughly investigated by persons independent of those who received and executed the order. The FCM should have systems to track disputes with customers, other brokers, as well as exchanges and clearinghouses. The resolution of such disputes should be summarized and reported to management.

Compliance Risk

Compliance risk is the risk to earnings or capital arising from violations of, or non-conformance with, laws, rules, regulations, prescribed practices, or ethical standards. Compliance risk also arises in situations where the laws or rules governing certain bank products or activities of the bank's clients may be ambiguous or untested. This risk exposes the institution to fines, civil money penalties, payment of damages, and the voiding of contracts. Compliance risk can lead to a diminished reputation, reduced franchise value, limited business opportunities, lessened expansion potential, and lack of contract enforceability.

National banks engaged in FCM activities through operating subsidiaries may be subject to increased compliance risk because of the bank's obligation to ensure compliance with laws and regulations issued by the OCC and the CFTC, in addition to rules of the NFA and the futures exchanges. The failure of a FCM to comply with applicable laws and regulations could result in enforcement action by one or more of these regulatory bodies. Noncompliance with applicable laws could also result in customer litigation with the FCM or the bank.

Domestic FCMs must comply with the CEA and regulations issued by the CFTC. The CFTC has delegated registration authority to the NFA, a self-regulatory organization which all domestic FCMs must join. Exchange member FCMs are also subject to any examination and reporting requirements imposed by the rules of a particular exchange and annual examinations by the NFA or a relevant futures exchange.

Some trade practice rules are meant to reduce the possibility of customer fraud. These include prohibitions on trades that are not clearly linked with an order (or a pre-specified bundled order), prohibitions on dual trading (unless some strict audit trail standards can be met by an exchange), and record-keeping rules (which are addressed below). During the open outcry, traders in the pits are actively bidding or offering orders which they hold. Where dual trading is allowed, these orders can be either for customers or for the floor broker's proprietary account. A prohibition of dual trading means that members trading for their own accounts cannot also bid and offer customers' orders on the same day.

Price manipulation is yet another issue addressed by trade practice rules. Under the CEA, price discovery is explicitly recognized as an important function of the futures markets. Therefore, any change in the auction rules is assessed relative to its impact on the accuracy of price discovery and the possibility for price manipulation.

Compliance Risk Management Practices

To ensure compliance with OCC guidance and other rules and regulations, the FCM should have a well-defined compliance program. FCMs should adopt sound policies and procedures including compliance manuals or other written documentation governing compliance matters. Procedures should also be adopted to ensure that manuals are updated periodically.

At a minimum, the FCM should have a designated compliance officer who is responsible for compliance with customer protection rules. Similar to the audit function, compliance officers should report independently of FCM management and demonstrate the necessary expertise to ensure compliance with rules and regulations governing FCM activities. Within the compliance function, management should designate an individual to handle customer complaints and inquiries. Management should set standards for disclosure of risks to customers that fully comply with exchange rules and adequately protect the FCM from charges of unfair treatment. In particular, the compliance system should ensure that the firm has a mechanism to assure that employees are familiar with applicable CFTC regulations and exchange rules.

Specifically, compliance should ensure that:

- Each customer account is reviewed on a periodic basis.

- Customer complaints are tracked and responded to.

- Customers receive required risk disclosure statements.

- All transactions and payments occurring in customer accounts are appropriate and authorized by the customer.

Finally, employees should receive ethics training that stresses honest, fair dealing practices which are in the best interest of the customer.

To further reduce compliance risk, bank management should ensure that bank subsidiary FCM activities are conducted in accordance with any conditions imposed by the OCC in its approval letter and in conformity with relevant OCC guidelines. At a minimum, this includes procedural controls, position or limits, and accounting methods consistent with those discussed in OCC Banking Circular 277, with appropriate tests to evaluate them on an ongoing basis.

A FCM should maintain capital sufficient to support customer and affiliate commitments, in addition to its own. The CFTC has established minimum financial requirements for FCMs, which require maintenance of adjusted net capital at certain identified levels. Exchanges may also impose minimum capitalization requirements. (The rules and regulations governing activity on foreign exchanges may differ substantially from domestic exchange rules. Management should be aware of these different rules and understand their impact on its ability to control risk.)

1. To evaluate the adequacy of board and senior management oversight of FCM activities.

2. To identify the levels of strategic, reputation, credit, liquidity, transaction, and compliance risk.

3. As applicable, to identify the level of price risk arising from proprietary trading activities. (Refer to the booklet entitled "Risk Management of Financial Derivatives" of the Comptroller's Handbook).

4. To communicate findings to the board and management and, as applicable, to obtain necessary commitments.

5. To ensure the supervisory strategy is appropriate.

Examination Planning

1. Based upon the OCC supervisory strategy approved for the bank, establish the scope of the FCM examination and determine necessary resources.

2. Obtain the following:

   □ Bank documents. (See appendix entitled "Sample FCM Request Letter.")
   □ OCC documents:

   — OCC approvals.
   — FCM filings.
   — Previous examination reports.
   — Overall summary comments.
   — Workpapers from previous examinations.

3. Using the information obtained in procedures 1-2:

   • Assess the nature of the FCM's activities. Determine whether the FCM functions as a:

   — Non-member FCM (executes and clears through other FCMs).
   — Non-clearing exchange member FCM (executes transactions but is not a clearinghouse member).
   — Clearing member (executes transactions and is a clearinghouse member).

   • Assess the nature of the FCM's customer base. Determine whether the FCM generally:

   — Takes orders, executes and/or clears for bank customers only.
   — Takes orders, executes and/or clears for customers with no banking relationship.
   — Takes orders, executes and/or clears for affiliates.
   — Takes orders, executes and/or clears for its own proprietary account(s).

- Identify significant changes since the previous examination with respect to:

    — Management.
    — Products and activities.
    — Customer base.
    — Exchange membership.
    — Risk measurement.
    — Back office operations and systems.
    — Policies and procedures.
    — Staffing.
    — Audit.

4. Prioritize issues for follow-up during the examination. Identify key weaknesses noted by audit, compliance, risk control, or previous examination reports concerning:

    - Oversight.
    - Risk measurement.
    - Risk control.
    - Risk limits.
    - Earnings and capital.
    - Compliance.
    - Operations and internal controls.

5. Where applicable, adjust the scope of the examination to build upon the supervisory work performed by other regulatory bodies. Document which OCC procedures have not been performed because another futures or options supervisory authority recently performed similar work.

Board and Senior Management Oversight

6. Determine whether significant policies directing the activities of FCM management are approved by the parent bank's board. Determine whether FCM policies and procedures promote consistency with the parent bank's stated risk appetite. At a minimum, determine whether such policies and procedures address:

    - Approved products.
    - Authorized activities.
    - Sales, marketing, and advertising.
    - Training.
    - Transactions with affiliates.
    - New product or activity approval.
    - Risk measurement methodologies.

- Risk limits (credit, liquidity, transaction, etc.).
- Limit exception approval.
- Validation of risk measurement tools.
- Stress testing of positions.
- Internal controls.
- Compliance and risk control.

7. Review the risk control function and staffing. Determine whether it:

   - Reports independently of individuals directly responsible for executing trades.
   - Is adequately staffed with qualified individuals.
   - Is fully supported by the board and senior management and has sufficient stature within the organization to be effective.
   - Has been provided with the technical and financial resources, corporate visibility, and authority to ensure effective oversight.

8. Assess the quality and stability of earnings. Consider:

   - Primary revenue sources.
   - Significant expenses.
   - Reimbursements or settlements made to customer accounts.
   - Fines or assessments by exchanges.
   - Unusual or extraordinary items.
   - Board approved risk/return objectives.
   - Existing and proposed levels of risk (credit, liquidity, operations, etc.).

9. Assess the quality of capital management. Consider:

   - Compliance with net capital requirements (exchange rules).
   - Activities/condition of affiliates.
   - Board stated objectives.
   - Adequacy of risk control, compliance and audit functions.
   - Concentrations.
   - Lines of credit (drawn upon and unused).
   - Debt/equity ratio.

10. Evaluate the quality of key personnel. Determine whether management is technically qualified and capable of properly engaging in the activity transacted by the FCM. Consider:

    - Management and staff education/experience.
    - Personnel turnover.
    - Job descriptions.
    - Adequacy of existing and projected support staff, considering projected volumes and types of transactions.

- Workload for operations personnel, considering use of overtime and level of transaction processing or reconciling errors.

11. Review management information systems (MIS) used to report to board members of the FCM and parent bank. Determine whether:

   - Systems support timely reporting of risk and return information.
   - Information reported to senior management and the board is accurate.
   - Management has taken raw risk measurement data and successfully transformed it into reports to the board that convey meaningful information about risk.

12. Determine whether the FCM has contingency plans that describe actions to be taken in times of market disruptions. Determine whether such plans address, at a minimum:

   - Management responsibilities.
   - Cash flow liquidity.
   - The deterioration of customer credit quality.

13. Evaluate transactions with affiliates and confirm that such transactions are conducted consistent with board-approved policies.

14. Review the audit scope for frequency and completeness. Determine whether the audit function includes the following checks:

   - Periodic review of FCM policies, limits, internal controls, and procedures.
   - Testing of operations functions including:

      — Transaction and confirmation controls.
      — Verification of balances held with clearinghouses, settlement agents, etc.
      — Verification of segregated funds held for customers.
      — Review of receipt and payment controls.
      — Accuracy of management reporting.

   - Review of brokerage costs and commissions, testing for accuracy.
   - Independent verification of the accuracy of pricing models and risk measurement methodologies.
   - Evaluation of internal controls and segregation of duties.

15. Determine the adequacy and qualifications of the audit staff size. Consider:

- Product complexity.
- Technical skills.
- Systems resources.

16. Assess the effectiveness of the audit process in ensuring internal controls are maintained and systems remain reliable. Consider:

    - Material criticisms or deficiencies.
    - Timely implementation of corrective actions.
    - Meaningful reporting to FCM senior management and the bank's board.

17. Determine whether the bank's board adequately holds management accountable for performance. Consider:

    - The consistency of performance against strategic and financial objectives over time.
    - Internal and external audit results.
    - The level of compliance with policies, procedures, and limits.
    - The quality and timeliness of communication to the board.

Strategic Risk

18. Evaluate the strategic and tactical business plans for the FCM. Consider:

    - The reasonableness of assumptions.
    - Any inconsistencies with board stated plans and risk tolerances.
    - The ability of existing resources to support planned expansion of activities.
    - Any potential changes in risk profile that may result from the implementation and/or achievement of planned strategies.

Reputation Risk

19. Review compensation plans, especially incentive compensation plans. Ensure that such plans:

    - Are designed to attract and retain appropriate talent.
    - Do not encourage employees to take unacceptable levels of financial risk (credit, price, liquidity).
    - Are consistent with the long-term strategic goals of the parent bank.
    - Do not encourage sales or transaction processing practices that might damage the reputation of the FCM or parent bank.

20. Determine that the FCM has procedures that address handling customer orders with specific restrictions (e.g., limits orders, stop orders, etc.).

21. Evaluate the potential loss posed by outstanding customer complaints, regulatory investigations, and pending litigation.

22. Determine whether sales and marketing practices are consistent with risk/return objectives set forth by the board. Consider:

    - Targeted customers.
    - Products/services promoted.
    - Training provided to sales and operations personnel.

Credit Risk

23. Review the organization structure to determine whether there is proper segregation between the credit function and marketing, execution, and margin payment/receipt functions.

24. Evaluate whether credit risk staff demonstrates knowledge of the products brokered by the FCM and possess an understanding of current and potential credit exposures.

25. Evaluate the adequacy of credit risk management policies and procedures. Determine whether the credit policies:

    - Establish limits for credit risk (credit quality, concentrations, tenors, etc.)
    - Require periodic credit reviews, risk ratings, credit exposure reporting, and limit exception notification.
    - Define the method used to calculate credit risk exposure and require periodic validation of the method.
    - Establish a process for limit exception approval and reporting.

26. Determine the adequacy of margin policies approved by the FCM. Consider:

    - The adequacy and compliance with exchange rules of initial margin requirements.
    - The amount and frequency of maintenance margin calls.
    - Types of acceptable margin.
    - Net versus gross margins.
    - Affiliate accounts.
    - Customer accounts with significant margins.

27. Verify that the FCM performs a review of the credit and operating risk of each exchange and clearing organization before it seeks membership therein.

28. Discuss with management the credit standards employed by the FCM in its customer selection process. Determine whether the standards address, at a minimum, a determination of a customer's:

   - Financial strength and liquidity.
   - Risk management objectives (speculating versus hedging, income stabilization versus capital preservation, etc.).
   - Knowledge and ability to understand the risks of sophisticated transactions.

29. If the FCM provides investment advisory services, determine whether the FCM obtains customer information as needed or as would reasonably be expected to be relevant to enable the FCM to evaluate the appropriateness of its advice to the customer.

30. If the FCM clears omnibus accounts, determine whether the FCM has credit standards that require the originating FCM to maintain sufficient liquidity and capital. (Sufficient liquidity and capital should protect the clearing FCM from a failure of the originating FCM which was caused by the default of one or more of the customers included in the omnibus account.)

31. If the FCM permits customers to use give-up brokers, determine whether the FCM has alternative controls to compensate for the inability of the FCM to review orders before execution.

32. If the FCM clears its trades through another FCM, determine whether the bank subsidiary FCM has established credit standards for approval of clearing FCMs. (These standards should protect the bank subsidiary FCM from losses arising from the use of its margin held by the clearing FCM to cover defaults by other customers of the clearing FCM.)

33. Determine whether the FCM sets credit limits for each customer and, at a minimum, whether the limits address:

   - The financial capacity (liquidity and net worth) of the customer.
   - Initial and maintenance margin levels.
   - Type of margin accepted.
   - Type, volume, and tenor of instruments executed or cleared.

34. Determine whether FCM credit policies address credit limit allocation (suballocation) and credit exposure aggregation for customers who execute trades on different exchanges or within different jurisdictions. Determine whether policies address:

   - The legal risks associated with executing transactions governed by foreign law.

- The potential lack of transparency.
- The correlation, or lack thereof, of market movements among various exchanges or jurisdictions.

35. Determine how FCM account officers verify credit exposure when orders are received. Consider issues such as:

   - Whether line approvals have product and tenor restrictions.
   - How transactions are approved for customers lacking a pre-approved line.
   - How credit exceptions are approved.

36. Review the credit risk measurement method used to estimate credit exposure to determine whether it adequately assesses current and potential credit exposure. Assess whether:

   - The system recalculates variation margin as frequently as necessary to control risk.
   - The system is designed to protect the FCM from credit losses resulting from price moves so rapid that the FCM cannot obtain additional margin in a timely manner.
   - The frequency and process of collateral valuation is adequate.
   - The model has been reviewed and validated by an independent party.
   - Credit exposure calculations are performed or verified by an independent person or unit.
   - Credit exposure reports are updated and changed on the system on a timely basis.

37. If the FCM permits corporate customers to phone orders directly to the trading floor, determine whether the FCM has alternative controls to monitor risk such as conducting frequent transaction reviews or maintaining higher credit standards for such customers.

38. Verify that the FCM maintains credit reserves to cover expected losses.

39. Determine how FCM management identifies, monitors, and resolves accounts experiencing credit deterioration.

40. Draw a sample of customers. Review credit files for:

   - Evidence that the FCM made all required disclosures.
   - Instances of additional disclosures provided to give customers comprehensive and timely information for making informed decisions.
   - Documentation that supports an adequate assessment of the appropriateness of the decision.

- Accurate and timely risk ratings.
- Reasonable customer limits.

41. Ascertain whether credit practices require:

    - Independent monitoring of aggregate credit exposure for each customer (including all credit exposure arising in other business lines) and comparison with limits.
    - An annual appropriateness review of account positions and transactions to ensure activity is consistent with account objectives.
    - Procedures to monitor:

        — Cumulative losses.
        — Daily trading volume relative to the balance of collateral in the account.
        — Naked short options.
        — Pre-screening orders from customers if necessary due to the style or trading or the creditworthiness of the customer.

42. Review reports received by senior management pertaining to credit risk. Determine whether the reports are:

    - Provided to the appropriate levels of management and the board.
    - Cover these issues in a comprehensive manner:

        — Portfolio credit quality information.
        — Concentrations.
        — Significant exposures.
        — Trend information (credit quality, tenor, etc.).
        — Normal market conditions versus stressed market conditions.

    - Accurate in terms of data integrity and address the impact of risk measurement assumptions or data aggregations.

Liquidity Risk

43. Evaluate the adequacy of liquidity risk policies and procedures. Determine whether the policies:

    - Establish liquidity limits (e.g., products, tenors, concentrations, activities, cash flow mismatches, open interest).
    - Require periodic reviews of liquidity risk exposures.
    - Require periodic cash flow analyses.
    - Establish processes for limit exception approvals and reporting.
    - Establish guidelines for parent bank and affiliate transactions.

44. Determine whether limits and reported exposures are derived consistently.

45. Determine the effectiveness of controls and the monitoring of risk limits. Liquidity controls should include:

   - The preparation and distribution of reliable liquidity reports containing accurate information.
   - Timely notification of actual or probable limit exceptions.
   - Prompt approval of all limit exceptions.
   - Monitoring and tracking of limit breaks and exception approvals.

46. Evaluate trends in cash flow liquidity over time. Consider management's ability to manage the inflow of margin received from customers as compared to the outflow of margin requirements to a clearing FCM or clearinghouse association. Focus evaluation on mismatched payments and settlements, and concentrations (e.g., customer, contract, exchange) and periods of market volatility.

Transaction Risk

47. If not included in information received from the request letter, gather the following items:

   - Flow charts of processing and reporting flows.
   - Systems policies and procedures.
   - Operations exceptions reports such as out-trades, uncollected fees/commissions, outstanding items, suspense items, miscellaneous losses, aging of margin calls.
   - Position reconcilements (customer aggregate-to-firm totals, clearinghouse totals).
   - Brokerage statements showing commissions, fees, give-ups, etc.
   - Disaster recovery plan.

48. Determine whether management has established comprehensive policies and procedures that set forth appropriate internal controls including:

   - Segregation of duties.
   - Trade entry and transaction documentation.
   - Confirmation.
   - Margin calculation.
   - Account statement.
   - Accounting treatment.
   - Management reporting.

49. Review the trade entry and processing environment to make sure the FCM has systems that:

- Limit access to trading systems.
- Ensure that all trades are promptly captured through the use of:

  - Pre-numbered tickets or sequential numbering systems.
  - Recorded telephone conversations.
  - Chronological records of telex/SWIFT messages.
  - Chronological records of margin calls.

- Ensure that sufficient transactional documentation supports limit reporting and a proper audit trail by determining that records of the original entry capture sufficient contract details, including:

  - Date and time the order was received (to the nearest minute).
  - Date and time the order was executed (to the nearest minute).
  - Name of the party executing the transaction.
  - Name of the party entering the transaction data.
  - Type of instrument, its price, and the amount.
  - Settlement or effective date.
  - Payment or settlement instructions.
  - Brokers' fees or commissions and other expenses.

- Reduce the likelihood of errors by reconciling individual positions to aggregate positions daily:

  - Front office to back office.
  - Aggregate position by instrument.
  - Customer and affiliate account records.
  - Aggregate account positions to clearinghouse records.

- Safeguard assets by establishing controls over the movement of cash, collateral, or other assets.
- Facilitate the tracking and correction of errors through the use of management information systems that monitor errors by the:

  - Party accepting the trade.
  - Party executing the trade.
  - Party entering the trade.
  - Settlement agent.

50. Determine whether the confirmation process requires that:

- Outgoing confirmations contain all relevant contract details.
- Outgoing confirmations are initiated no later than one business day after the transaction date, upon expiry or option exercise.

- The method of confirmation used provides a documentation trail — such as recorded telephone lines, paper confirmation, or telex/SWIFT messages — that supports the FCM's position in the event of disputes.
- Incoming confirmations are handled by persons independent of the employees who execute trades.
- All discrepancies requiring corrective action are promptly identified and acted upon.
- All discrepancies are tracked, aged, and reported to management and trends by type are identified and addressed.

51. Review margin calculations to assure the FCM records comply with exchange rules. If the FCM acts as clearing member, check that daily margin calculations agree with clearinghouse records.

52. Review reconcilements of deposits with clearing organizations and the valuation of assets on deposit.

53. Determine that the FCM has procedures to monitor, analyze, and resolve out-trades.

54. Obtain a list of suspense items due from/to customers. Investigate stale items and trends in these accounts.

55. Verify that the FCM has the following controls and procedures with respect to customer funds:

- Assets placed on deposit with banks, trust companies, clearing organizations, and other FCMs are:

    — Carried in accounts clearly identified as funds segregated for customers and,
    — The FCM has received an acknowledgment to that effect from each such depository.
- Total funds on deposit are reconciled on a daily basis.
- A daily calculation of total funds required by rule or regulation to be on deposit is performed.
- Customer statements are prepared listing:

    — Contracts with current price.
    — Unrealized profit and loss on open contracts.
    — The amount of any customers funds held.
    — A listing of transactions.
    — A detailed accounting of all charges and credits.

56. Determine that the FCM has procedures that ensure that customer funds are invested only as permitted by account authorization, law, rule, or

regulation.

57. Select a sample of customer account statements (including accounts with large positions, zero balances, and high volume). Trace positions, cash and margin to FCM account records to confirm that:

- Customer purchase/sale transactions are recorded accurately.
- Customer funds are properly segregated.
- Information concerning customer funds are properly disclosed.

58. Review exchange trade registers and confirmations from clearing brokers to account for trades executed.

59. Review the revaluation of securities posted as margin. Determine that key pricing parameters are obtained from, or verified by, a source independent of the traders and are representative of the market.

60. Obtain a flow chart of reporting and systems flows and identify important risk points:

- Review the policies and procedures governing MIS.
- Determine the adequacy of segregation of duties.

61. Review the personal computer policy for the institution, including controls over spreadsheet applications. Ensure that:

- Brokers cannot make changes to key spreadsheets for valuation or risk management purposes.
- Data and applications are protected.

62. Review current systems capabilities and planned upgrades or enhancements. Ensure that:

- Front office risk management requirements are properly considered.
- Systems planning and implementation schedules are consistent with transaction growth and the current and planned level of business activity.
- Security controls prevent unauthorized access to systems information.
- Contingency planning is acceptable.

63. Review functional applications of MIS such as credit administration, trade settlement, accounting, and risk control. Determine whether:

- The information is timely.
- The format supports management of risk.
- The information is accurate.

64. For reports to senior management, determine that they:

- Permit the FCM to track errors and miscellaneous losses in sufficient detail to identify the source of errors.
- Are prepared by individuals independent of traders.
- Reflect the current status and trends for the following items:

  — Aging of documentation exceptions.
  — Position reconcilements.
  — Outstanding general ledger reconciling items.
  — Uncollected funds due.
  — Unmatched trades.
  — Aging of unconfirmed trades.
  — Suspense items payable/receivable.
  — Brokerage payments.
  — Miscellaneous losses.

Compliance Risk

The following examination procedures highlight significant rules and regulations required by domestic futures and options regulatory authorities. The examiner may use these procedures, as applicable, to supplement examination work performed by the CFTC, SRO or exchange authorities.

65. Ensure the FCM has systems and controls that permit it to comply with regulations and rules governing its activities. Rules and regulations vary among exchanges and jurisdictions. Generally, rules will include the following requirements:

- Periodic computation of minimum financial requirements. (For example, see CFTC Rule 1.17, 17 CFR 1.17).
- Daily computation of customer segregation requirements. (For example, see CEA 4d(2) and CFTC Rule 1.20, 17 CFR 1.20).
- Daily computation of cash, securities, or other customer assets used to satisfy obligations to foreign futures and foreign options exchanges. (For example, see CFTC Rule 30.7, 17 CFR 30.7).
- Reporting requirements, audited regulatory reports, and other required filings. (For example, see Form 1-FR, CFTC Rule 1.10, 17 CFR 1.10).
- Segregation requirements of foreign regulators.

66. Determine that the FCM provides for accountants' reports as required by regulations and rules governing its activities. (For example, see CFTC Rule 1.16, 17 CFR 1.16). Accountant's reports should include a description of any material inadequacies as to accounting systems,

accounting controls, and procedures for the safeguarding of customer assets. Review the audit letter, financials, and accompanying notes. Review reports on meetings between the accountants and FCM management regarding internal controls.

67. Determine whether the FCM has adopted procedures that ensure:

   - Confidentiality of customer account information.
   - Fair treatment of customers:

     — If the FCM acts in a dual capacity (executing for customers as well as for its own account or for the account of affiliates), determine that the interest of customers, including the use of or access to information, and their transactions, have priority over the interests of the FCM and its affiliates. (For example, see CFTC Rule 155, 17 CFR 155).
     — Among customers, each account is treated impartially with equal access to information and priority of execution.

68. Ensure that the FCM has designated a compliance officer who is responsible for handling and responding to customer complaints and inquiries. Determine that the firm has controls or procedures to assure that:

   - Account officers cannot intercept customer complaints or inquiries and that all complaints or inquiries are routed to the compliance officer.
   - Compliance officers periodically review tape recordings of conversations between customers and associated persons, or order clerks, if made.

69. Determine whether the firm maintains a compliance procedures manual or other written documentation outlining compliance matters.

70. Verify that the FCM has a process for informing appropriate personnel of changes to regulations and exchange rules.

71. Determine whether the FCM has procedures to ensure that each customer account is reviewed periodically to check that:

   - All transactions have been authorized by the customer before execution.
   - If applicable, the approval of customers authorizing the FCM to execute transactions without prior specific approval is documented in writing.
   - All required risk disclosures are made.

- Account statements accurately reflect the current status of the account and reflect all transactions.

72. Determine whether the compliance officer or other supervisory personnel reviews the propriety of commission payments.

73. Determine whether the compliance officer or other supervisory officer reviews all promotional material before it is first used.

74. If the bank subsidiary FCM carries accounts for employees of other FCMs, determine whether:

    - The bank subsidiary FCM obtains written authorization from appropriate parties at such other FCMs.
    - Copies of customer statements are forwarded to such other FCM. (See CFTC Rule 155.3(c).)

75. If the FCM allows its employees to maintain accounts with other firms, determine whether the FCM has procedures to authorize and monitor such activity, including conducting a review of the employees' account statement and order tickets. (See CFTC Rule 155.3(d)).

Conclusions

76. Use the information and analysis prepared throughout the examination to draw conclusions about the levels of strategic, reputation, credit, liquidity, transaction, and compliance risks.

77. Use the information and analysis prepared throughout the examination to draw conclusions about the adequacy of board and senior management oversight of strategic, reputation, credit, liquidity, transaction, and compliance risks.

78. Discuss findings with senior management and board members at exit meetings. As applicable, obtain necessary commitments for corrective action.

79. Prepare report comments and internal analysis comments, as appropriate.

80. Update the bank's supervisory strategy.

Yes   No

1. Does the board and senior management provide adequate oversight of FCM activities?

2. Has the board approved policies and procedures that are consistent with stated risk tolerances?

3. Do risk measurement systems identify and accurately reflect levels of strategic, reputation, credit, liquidity, transaction, and compliance risks?

4. Do existing management information systems provide the board and senior management with accurate and timely information?

5. Are control deficiencies that have been identified by audit, compliance, or other regulatory bodies promptly addressed and resolved?

6. Do margin policies and practices adequately protect the FCM from unwarranted credit or liquidity risk?

7. Do internal controls and systems used in FCM operations limit exposures that might negatively affect the bank's financial condition and/or reputation?

Sample FCM Request Letter

The following provides guidance to the examiner preparing for an onsite examination of a FCM operating subsidiary. Consistent with OCC policy, the examiner should use existing bank management reports whenever possible and keep to a minimum reports that bank management must prepare specifically for the examiner. Additionally, examiners should only request items in this list applicable to the risks to be evaluated during the examination. For example, if examiners will rely on work performed by another regulatory body to evaluate compliance risk, they may not need to request item 11.

NOTE: Copies need not be made of items marked by an asterisk. Examiners will review originals and return them to bank management during the examination.

_____   *1.   Registration data filed with the NFA, OCC.

_____   2.   Summary of FCM activities (non-member, executing member, clearing member, etc.).

_____   3.   List of types of futures and options on futures contracts transacted by the FCM.

_____   4.   As applicable, list of clearing FCMs through which the FCM executes or clears trades.

_____   5.   As applicable, list of exchanges on which the FCM executes or clears trades.

_____   6.   As applicable, list of clearinghouses of which the FCM is a member.

_____   7.   Summary information reflecting how much of FCM's business is conducted for:

- Affiliate bank(s).
- Nonbank affiliates.
- Third-party customers.
- The FCM's own account.

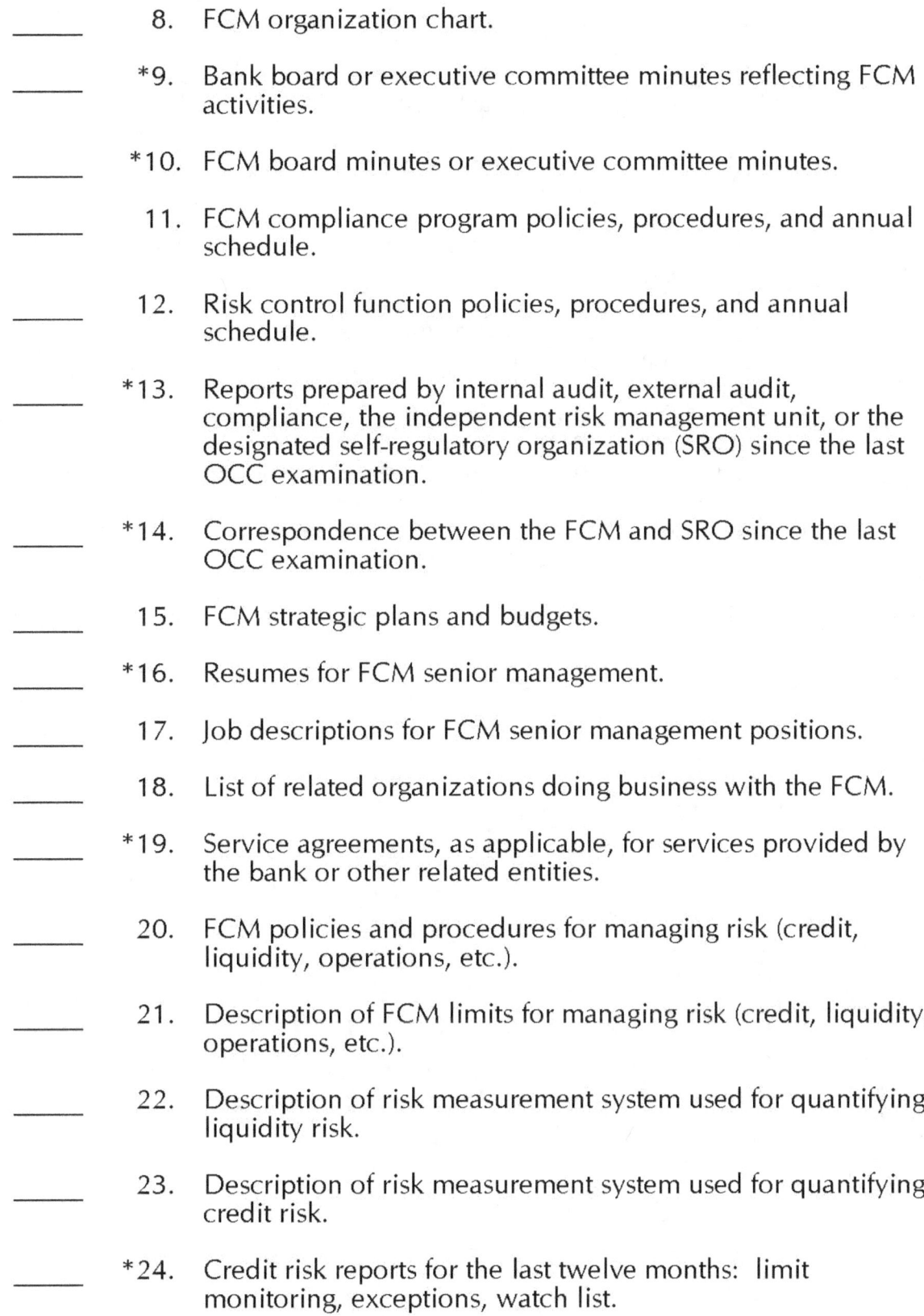

_____   8.   FCM organization chart.

_____   *9.   Bank board or executive committee minutes reflecting FCM activities.

_____   *10.   FCM board minutes or executive committee minutes.

_____   11.   FCM compliance program policies, procedures, and annual schedule.

_____   12.   Risk control function policies, procedures, and annual schedule.

_____   *13.   Reports prepared by internal audit, external audit, compliance, the independent risk management unit, or the designated self-regulatory organization (SRO) since the last OCC examination.

_____   *14.   Correspondence between the FCM and SRO since the last OCC examination.

_____   15.   FCM strategic plans and budgets.

_____   *16.   Resumes for FCM senior management.

_____   17.   Job descriptions for FCM senior management positions.

_____   18.   List of related organizations doing business with the FCM.

_____   *19.   Service agreements, as applicable, for services provided by the bank or other related entities.

_____   20.   FCM policies and procedures for managing risk (credit, liquidity, operations, etc.).

_____   21.   Description of FCM limits for managing risk (credit, liquidity, operations, etc.).

_____   22.   Description of risk measurement system used for quantifying liquidity risk.

_____   23.   Description of risk measurement system used for quantifying credit risk.

_____   *24.   Credit risk reports for the last twelve months: limit monitoring, exceptions, watch list.

_____ 25. Summary of compensation programs.

_____ *26. Actual compensation paid to senior managers and line officers for the last fiscal period.

_____ 27. FCM volume of activity reports since the last OCC examination.

_____ 28. FCM revenue and expense reports since the last OCC examination.

_____ *29. Key marketing presentations, sales documents, advertising materials.

_____ *30. Sales training information (manuals, etc.).

_____ *31. Reports used by management to monitor margin accounts.

_____ 32. List of any reimbursement or settlement made to customer accounts since the last OCC examination.

_____ *33. The FCM's net capital computations for the last 12 months.